Fluke Print

Jeffery Donaldson

FLUKE PRINT

POEMS

The Porcupine's Quill

Library and Archives Canada Cataloguing in Publication

Donaldson, Jeffery, 1960–, author
Fluke print : poems / Jeffery Donaldson.

ISBN 978-0-88984-411-7 (softcover)

I. Title.

PS8557.O527F58 2018 C811'.54 C2018-900519-X

1 2 3 • 20 19 18

Published by The Porcupine's Quill, 68 Main Street, PO Box 160, Erin, Ontario N0B 1T0. http://porcupinesquill.ca

Represented in Canada by Canadian Manda.
Trade orders are available from University of Toronto Press.

'Over Head', 'Fountain Pen' and 'Found in an Essay by Max Beerbohm' were previously published in the *Alabama Literary Review*. The author thanks William Thompson the editor and also acknowledges the support of the Ontario Arts Council.

We acknowledge the support of the Ontario Arts Council and the Canada Council for the Arts for our publishing program. The financial support of the Government of Canada is also gratefully acknowledged.

Canada Council for the Arts Conseil des arts du Canada
Canada
ONTARIO ARTS COUNCIL
CONSEIL DES ARTS DE L'ONTARIO
an Ontario government agency
un organisme du gouvernement de l'Ontario
Ontario
Ontario Media Development Corporation

For Karen Schindler

If a speck of dust should fall in her lap,
brush it away with your fingers:
and if there be nothing, brush away the nothing:
let that be a reason for you to serve her.

Ovid, *The Art of Love*

Table of Contents

ONE

Fluke Print

Barbara Howard, i.m.

After the water breaks, after the breach,
after the coming about and the time
for breathing, after the sunlight spangles

the top-wash and then the graceful sounding,
after the flukes slip through the water folds
hauling the glimpsed undergreens after them,

in the baffled quiet where the rift closes,
let a print, skimmed from under, circle round,
the polished nap's water-glossing water

unripple the jostling, flatten the gulped
vortex and curb the churning lees that skirt
the vanishing point still slipping away.

What were the chances of your being here
to watch the remnant aureole take shape,
this parting stillness in place of a wake?

Somewhere far below is the living thing.
Its flukes' drowsy rise-and-fall in the dark
swims out of its own form. Was it a waste

to leave behind this token? Let it be.
The disgorged placenta, not holding on,
not cleaving where the body slipped from it,

loosens the grip on its own whereabouts,
and slowly, as is becoming of water,
eases its own likeness into the sea.

Poem Whisperer

> *But all is changed, that high horse riderless,*
> *Though mounted in that saddle Homer rode …*
>
> —W.B. Yeats

Pegasus would never stoop
so low, old nag, shadow of yourself,
dead set in the far paddock,

ears laid back, unlistening,
eyes everywhere, the lines about
your neck and legs all confusion.

I have been getting nowhere
near you. The way you keep
to yourself, cagey and skittish,

back off when I so much
as lift a finger, the air
of a rough handling written

all over you. Too many
joyrides? You led by the nose?
You jammed through paces?

My only trick was to make you
think my move was your move.
You seemed to go with it.

The way you came around
without my telling, took apples
from me when I had them.

Remember the early days?
You were in high spirits, all about
the trees, anywhere you liked,

cut loose in the open, your antic
capers' Sapphic loops, leaping
round, ears spreading like fans.

A light snow is falling.
You look cold. You seem
not to be watching me.

But listen, there is word of an apple.
Come nearer and taste it.
I promise not to put you down.

Word for Tree

For John Terpstra

That was the day we brought
the sign with the word tree on it
to the tree in the middle of the field.
We gathered under the tree

holding the sign up. Some cheered
and were satisfied. Some walked away,
having hoped for more. A woman said,
thank you all for being here.

There were disagreements.
Should the sign hang from the tree,
or be placed on the ground before it?
Where should the word tree go?

A man in a tweed jacket mused,
perhaps an arrow on the sign
under the word tree should point
in the direction where the tree is.

Some brought other words, a the,
a tall, but were asked to be patient.
Many were still uncertain.
What if we're wrong? they asked.

After a while it grew later. A dark
came on to show it was evening.
One commented as the crowd thinned,
Can't blame them for trying,

and went away. Two volunteers
picked up the word sign's tree
and carried it from the field, upright,
so as not to spill any leaves.

Contrapuntal

Both ends of this dull pencil have their say
and go together. For when I try

the tapered point, finding I am led
to write out all its darker things, instead

I catch my eye ascending to the nub
(the nodding jester's blunt 'ah there's the rub!')

that daubs above the dismal lines below
a flourishing 'I would not have it so.'

Dyslexic, mute, it holds—that subtle curse—
a mirror up to nothing, in reverse.

My aching slant, my least that can be said,
is followed backwards by a nulling thread,

whose wavings-off, dismissive counter-sign,
become facetious, affable, benign,

a clear, upending scrub, as though
the baser word that everything must go

were giddily extinguished in the air.
What all I cannot say is written there.

Fountain Pen

I spread my blue privates
on the creaking line,
those aired unmentionables

showing wear. Scrawled
awkward tatters, so public,
so seen. The skid stains.

Higher up, an inky gloom
waiting in store will trickle
down, come evening,

turned like an hourglass,
and its obfuscations
will cover entire sheets.

Hang it all. Let the dark
empty. Come morning, I'll see
where the blues have run.

Man Filled with Questions

The man filled with questions
carried around the town a sheet
of paper on a clipboard. The word
dog was printed on it several times.

To the right of each word dog
there was an empty square
large enough to hold a checkmark.
He could hardly contain himself.

Then there was a dog who came
and sat down in front of him.
The man hurried to place a checkmark
in the first empty square.

He thought to himself, I am
just a man filled with questions,
but if I were the great scholar of being
these would be my findings.

GO

The 12:10 from Aldershot to Union,
the weather in its Sunday best, August
breezing the summer lights. The green doors close.

From my seat I hear, don't see, behind me
the pitched voices of three girls laughing
about guys and heartache, under-twenties

as I picture them, their each turn falling
over the last with more audacious story,
potty mouths testing a fallen innocence.

One says, 'I mean, it was three fucking years,
and I loved the guy, I fucking loved him,
but I'm not who he thought I was.' Another says,

'I don't know shit.' My mind comes and goes,
sifting the scraps of their carnal moxie
—'He followed me on Facebook!'—their sense

of the world as the safest place to be
themselves in. 'He's there with these other girls!
I know, isn't that fucked up? I'm like ...'

Don't. Don't finish that sentence. But I do.
And suddenly, like that, my eyes squeezed shut,
a boxcar in a station at Kraków,

early forties, three girls, whom I see
but cannot hear, huddle close, still as clouds,
clutching antique suitcases. The oldest one

whispers something inaudible, and the two
younger nod and look up to her, reassured.
A grotesque self-parody out of Dickens.

Am I really going there? ‘And he’s all …
“You and I are the same person,” and I’m like
“I don’t know what you’re doing, but *whatever*.”’

Why does this always happen? Stop it now.
But the train keeps coming, green paint peeling
on the wooden doors, the three girls pressed close,

their suitcases taken for safekeeping.
‘So I’m like, Ok I’ll go, but dude, you’re leaving *that*
right where it is.’ The two others giggle.

Their voices leap, latest besting the last
like fountains chasing after their own heights,
sun smacked, breaking off in splashed laughters.

But I’m too far gone. The oldest one lifts
the youngest in her arms, fixes a button
on her blouse. Just kill me now, I think.

If they get away in time, I’ll be all right.
Only one more station before Union
and we can part, go our separate ways,

and I can let the damned train—its couplings
pulling now every which way—recede at last,
and the three girls, beside themselves, huddling

as if their lives depended on it, in the end
be nowhere in sight, the green doors closing,
the platform almost empty. Last stop, thank god.

Do they even know where they are being taken,
assuming one could ever turn back and tell them,
and would they believe it? I hope not.

Some things are better left for the moment.
'"Dude, what do you take me for?" And he lifts
me up like this. And oh my god, I'm like....'

TWO

Apologia

True story. Guy meets girl, guy falls in love.
Not too fine a point on it, girl's lonely,
was hitched once, got up feeling hungry.

Guy's own marriage—honest—'s of that open sort,
New Agey thing, wife with another man:
they're friends, non-conjugal. Got the picture?

You hear crazy like that nowadays. Guy's free,
far's he knows, to be the fella a girl wants,
knows not to take more'n she wants to give.

Funny part, girl's a beauty, crazy smart,
real Helen of Troy, but she don't feel it.
Smarts do that to ya when the ledger's off.

She's told, now on, to figure different,
but kinda looks at him sideways, 'cause get this,
the guy's still payin' the bills, chez lui,

if you follow me, all kids and car pools,
lookin' after things. Don't that beat all.
He says, different kinds o' love, don't you see?

Girl's real smart, like I said, feels a fella
worth a kiss oughta make a choice,
and if he don't, makes her second fiddle.

Now *he's* in a spot, and well, he's thicker'n
potato soup, kinda throws up his hands,
paces back and forth, starts bellyachin'

’bout how things got backwards over time.
Now what answer is that? Get you only
so far, pleadin’ deer caught in the headlights.

He’s all, but I told ya how I shimmied
from the start! Lamppost with a burnt-out bulb
got more chance o’ changing hisself. Nothing

but his way of puttin’ it all back on her,
though he don’t say so. Ain’t no Sisyphus,
that girl. Can only roll a flat rock up

its own hill so long before she’ll stand straight
and let it roll back down. Which it don’t!
Just kinda lies there, like a rock, hopin’

she change her mind, come back and roll some more.
He’s all torn up too. Ain’t for me to say,
but if I were him … well, long story short.

Last Thinks

I

Time to make myself up and come to terms,
find the sound verbal formulas, conjure
a blessing. Try my hand at some of these.

And why not say what happened, make a start?
A Saturday-night do, you picked me out
of a hallway horde, helped me join the dots:

we had been in touch years ago by mail.
I thought you were much older, I recalled;
you laughed: I'd been aloof, peremptory.

The chiffon blouse you wore that night—almost
see-through, like yourself, not see-through at all—
said, you will never know how naked I am.

You were right. I was too shy to start something,
so to say goodbye, as in a poem like this,
I touched your elbow passing when I left.

II

Anguish, anger, remorse. Should I go on?
A prickly question. Tell me what to do
with ends remaining, dead ends, endless ends.

I take a hunk of raw desire that burns,
a love that is for no one else but you,
a scalding ache that storms each addled thought,

and make a (metaphor) small box for them,
called things like Surely Better This Way, or
I Saw This Coming, or I Am to Blame,

then tape it shut and put it somewhere safe,
go out for an evening, movie with friends.
Maybe try a date, stay out the whole night!

There it will be when I get home, the box
with all those things I can leave behind me
without fearing that I've lost what I've lost.

IV

Other things not so easy to return
are returned without our knowing. I guessed
before I arrived. The moment you said

'Let's not be in touch, lie low for a while'
and closed your door, my head filled with cotton.
Empty feelings struggled to make room

for what they already were. I made it
to a Tim's drive-through, where a woman's voice,
Delphian Sybil, asked, 'May I help you?'

Things you would think impossible to return
simply go back to their source. Think of how,
for a cloud, just being itself becomes

a burden, the way ahead clear. Its task:
let go the weight that makes it what it is
without turning back. Small double-double.

V

After years of neglect, your heart had learned
its manners and memorized the classics.
Feelings were best coolly thought about.

It somehow explained your ardour's double-take.
Winters, when I took off my scarf and boots
and sat down beside you, all energy,

I felt your need keep clear of my style.
It stayed out of things, the way a child
clings to the mother's skirt, shy, unafraid,

certain the elders do all the talking.
But there were hints too of a private life,
elfish and unruled, that included me

in ways I missed. All pleasantries endured,
the child is sent outdoors, where it runs now
over the snow, waving my scarf in the wind.

VI

The first time I saw you, Karen, I felt
I would never tire of drinking from you.
You were at a loss what to do with my urge,

but let me kiss parts you were shy about,
under your arms, the arch of your foot,
the tapering lapse below your navel.

You never made a sound. I've decided
that memories are thoughts about something.
Those winter and summer evenings

we were apart, I thought of the love-hours,
the ones already past—gripping and spent—
the ones looked forward to. They went through me.

They are the same thought, I thought: what was
and what will be. Yes, what was once will now
be me curled in bed alone with your name.

VII

The way you gentled your hand on the back
of my head and held it left me feeling
as though no one had done that in my life.

No one had. My fat head drowns in deafening
rackets. But your hand was a shushing hand.
It said, I will cradle you. It said, there now.

It said as well all I knew about how,
fetching, love might hold me harmless, a hand
on the back of a head. One giddy night,

we played a game and each thought to ourselves
of one thing the other did that we loved.
I said, in any case I wouldn't dare

spoil it by telling. You held them up
as though you were stumped: open, withholding,
the idea of wonder in your empty hands.

VIII

The *principle of hope*, Ernst Bloch believed,
is a forward-dawning. The Buddha says
nothing arises. Can't make up my mind.

Those mornings when I awoke by your side
the sun was already up, and you, snug,
unrisen, were the warm place we entered.

Though I had turned and drifted off, you stayed
near me through the night, showed how following
your dreams was a way of waiting for me.

Nothing can arise, because no thing is
truly here, the Buddha vows, that has not
been here all along. Like you at my side,

like the way an openness waits to be
entered by being open, the way that
waking with you was a forward-dawning.

IX

It can take time to notice a woman
often keeps herself at bay, and accept
it's not a small part of why you love her.

In you, I found a crux to go looking for.
To my delight, you kept excluding yourself,
every day more certain of my anguish.

You would come to bed, a purloined letter,
hiding your nakedness in plain view,
as though to say, Wysiwyg, I'm right here.

Look at me. And I would. And we would
play Catch Me If You Can, or Hide and Seek,
or Blind Man's Buff. I loved falling for it.

It was like Lucy holding the football
for Charlie Brown: her inviting look,
and his confidence in being fooled again.

X

I read this morning that a photograph
is a picture of something you once lost
and lost at once. Truth be told, I possess

so many of you. You're always cagey
about your mugs, say No to most of them:
wrong smile, wrong mood. We never agreed.

There was a time, such half tones in a pouch
came tucked with their own transparencies,
as like you as not: whole strips of your face

in stark contrast, your black-and-white's flip-side
palette of opposing greys. Where to find
what I've lost, or where to find *that* I've lost?

One day, in a dark room, I held you up
to the light, asking, Are you the shadow
I saw as my opposite? Negative.

XI

I never gazed at you like an artist,
never stood, quiet as a camera,
and watched you, seated, towel your back dry,

then your neck, while you knew and didn't know.
You were always slipping under covers,
as though somehow you weren't perfect.

Just like me to say I could never draw.
You undressed, you skin-deep modelling
yourself after the unwatched bather,

offering, for a time to come, the look
of your breasts in the sketcher's eye, given
it was yours to give. Seizing the moment

from her unfixed air turned slightly away,
he must block out the few lines he will need
to make *Nu à la baignoire* when she's gone.

III

Why are the gifts of love impermanent?
'Return to Sender' outdoes 'Please Forward'
at the parting hour. The easy ones first:

letters and love cards, two snazzy shirts,
a secret-hollow book, poems sewn by hand,
a noteworthy fountain pen, silver grey.

I have a small box in mind to put them in.
The pen as well? I hold it in my hand.
You make a gift of helping others make.

I picture you exploring a glass case.
I'll take this one, you would have said,
thinking of me. How the ungiven-back

keeps giving back what is no longer given,
the way ink always runs behind, the way
knowing we're done still needs to be written.

XII

Six years of mental strife. In the good sense.
A marriage of true minds marries the grind.
William Blake pleaded that it's all we have,

lending an ear to the Old German *strīdan*,
its tapped word root learning to strive in strife,
as we did. Well, we put up a good fight,

neither of us suited to the loud cry.
We were trying to figure each other out:
the mess I make of things in every way,

your pains for detail. We couldn't have been
more at odds. Was the passion in spite
or because of it? We grappled, we strove.

Our lovemaking was full of seizures
and ransacks. Our bodies squabbled,
each insisting, I must change your life.

XIII

We got around to the spooning after.
'I'm turning in.' And you would roll over,
and I took your side, as long as I could.

Always the something that lay between us.
But think how streams find a given eddy
and whirl with it, curl around the inward

bends and momentums, circle their widenings,
spin their contours throughout, a casting off
and out again. How your water opened

was a mystery, curves abreast, your lapse
that pulled me down and in by rushing
at its own hollows while they deepened.

We kept thinking we were the wrong way round.
All the while the truest bond that held us
was a gap that flowed through us and away.

XIV

One day, without thinking, I let it fall
that arriving I felt a heaviness,
like putting on a hefty coat: the weight

of your innocent expectation, my need
to be such and such. I'd hoped to confide,
but you were hurt. Too late to walk it back.

Your idea of love made the gravity
at your core, weighty and pulling inward.
I felt it draw things to itself, like me.

The thing about a fundamental force,
our science says, it doesn't hold you down
or back, so much as pass, the way light can,

through you on its way to somewhere else.
Or someone. Even adrift as I am,
I feel the crushing acceleration.

XV

Let your last thinks all be thanks, said Wystan Hugh.
I've tried. I think of your voice. Your hands.
Your expression at the door when you opened.

Your posture did me in. I would picture
the arc of a slender reed in a breeze.
How to be thankful for gone loves? Takes time.

Straight afterwards, the losing makes you feel
the reed, for instance, grow small in your mind,
as though it were drifting away from you

as it drifts away from you. Gratitude
has its limits. To be near the merging
of was and isn't and still feel much obliged.

Isn't *was* what 'last thinks' already means?
To open my hands and say *Good of you*.
Auden meant dying, of course, not love.

XVI

Monks in their cells make vows of abstinence
to make a point. 'My body is nothing.
I lay it aside in deference to You.'

They rise from need, exiled and austere,
and draw rings around a sanctity,
where not being themselves they come to be.

Their nearest nearness to the name of God:
I am not that I am. I know that, but
fold it backwards, the abstinence that is.

The slow touch of you was sacred to me:
your mouth, your taste, your hair like a manna,
the small of your back when you pressed towards,

and how you curled to the side afterwards.
Promise me this one thing, if I give up
all other love, that we were what we were.

XVII

Time to do the old man, I think to myself,
hang up the jock support, talk the good game
of Buddhist solitude, awake at dawn,

turn Eros palliative. You're bound to feel
that way out of the hurt, I'm told. Just wait.
But surely there comes an actual point

when your body loses taste for the scrum,
the warm scrimmage after the feminine
hush-hush. Your unfathomable occult.

Something as tangible as how you turned
your wrist, tasted wine, or would leave out
certain fingers when you held a bowl.

Ah, the difference between wanting *it*
and wanting you. Come to me one more time,
my temptress, my nurse, and put me to bed.

XVIII

In our last talk you came out with it.
'I didn't give you everything, because
—do I need to say it?—neither did you.'

It was a cold matter of trust, you said.
If that were in earnest, neither of us
would have folded. Always the give-and-take:

you needed the thing that I had to give;
I needed you to need it, given what I had.
There was a fullness in that, an All-in.

Your reserve was everything to me.
It meant I could keep trying. What I saw,
I adored. If you were not wholly there,

if there was more to me than you possessed,
a missing word, a gesture, a way to be,
I think each of us was the more deceived.

XIX

I would talk up my gift for solitude
and left you to take it personally.
At your tether's end, you let me have it.

Trouble was: being around another
not myself, always thinking I should think
for two, took it out of me. I conjured

empty rooms—like the one I'm sitting in—
free to picture you, genius apart,
unwantingly grown painfully wanted.

But that other seclusion: how nights you
left me alone inside you, and knowing
I was there, trusting, you went off as well,

and I listened for the moment you came
back and proved how solitude was *your* gift,
not mine. I was that close to losing it.

XX

That damned Proust, what help is he now I want
to love someone actual, not recalled?
Loss is desire in its final form.

I'll say this. Being not liked, in the end,
hurts more than being, all those years with you,
not like, the way I always bragged we weren't.

You hung in for ages, defended us
to others and yourself, took your head
to heart, ran headlong at my deficits.

For what? The dry crumbs of my wanting you
that Proust jeered you can't help but stoop and pick,
thinking it is who you are? Then all at once

you are free of it, discover you can
do without, and have the strength to leave me
with your loss, as though I desired nothing but.

XXI

The future past, grammar's most hopeful tense.
When we quarrelled, neither of us wanted
the final word. I would wait for you

to speak, and you me, hoping there was more.
We muddled along with things not working
because they worked. At least the muddling did.

Would it have changed if we'd continued on,
made astringent feel like euphoria,
and learned how to make friends with lack?

Would we gain more than we already have,
just by having it once more? It may be
looking forward to a remembered past

is loss's way of staying in touch. I choose
the poem that, out of love, will stop dead,
and leave the last thought that goes after you.

Copula

Among our parsing, several moods
of selfhood, conjugated thus—
I am, you are, she is, word-chess
where grapple our twinned solitudes,

where all our spoked divergent lines
of empathy come to quarrel—
we seek a marriage of true Mines
in the first-person plural.

First person? Plural? *We* won't add up.
The pronoun buckles under weight.
Our one-for-two's an iffy trope,
dichotomous and incomplete

unless made whole by that pure *is*,
the metaphoric predicate,
whose blithe between-where synapses
can couple kinds, make this a that.

Sooner said than done. Lying alike
conjoined, subjects that in part agree,
we give it the old college try,
our both I's open, cheek to cheek,

and listen, knowing how, just when
you touch your inner, stranger half,
my me divides you from yourself,
but seeks you there, again, again.

How else to conjugate, or dance
our *pas de deux* of Her and His,
to merge and part, on the off chance
(however wrong) we is, we is.

Translation of an Unwritten Love Poem

Lovers of the gloss say it would be
nothing to catch your drift, lay hands on
a like word for your differences,

beguile with a flourish *débonnaire*
your hints and gists, your givens,
and put the naked original to bed.

But you were having none of it,
knew that however I took you
to say what you meant, there were still

the gestures alone, the long walks
at Springbank walked in silence,
the thousand unremembered kisses,

and the hand resting on my shoulder
as of someone there no matter what,
if only I had said as much.

Nones

That late afternoon I fell asleep
with your nipple in my mouth.
When I awoke, you were still there,
my tongue spooning it.

I remember how quiet it was.
You have this exquisite give
you keep to yourself. So that's one thing.
The other is that you let me sleep.

Metaphors of Love
Are Like What You Make Them

My mouth on the peachy
lapse below your navel:
a solitary canoe dips blind
on the moonlit lake.

At every turn your shoulder
feints from that easement
downward toward the breast:
not one cloud over the hills.

Your neck slenders
into the niche behind your ear:
only gravity can lift down
the apple from the branch.

As I Bend Towards You

Stay with me now. The greyed river
flowed from itself but could not empty
itself empty. Always more to be flowed from

kept flowing. That is the wrong way
to empty yourself, said the patient sea.
My emptiness is a form of magnitude.

I am its source. In me you may come
to nothing. Let my vacant body rise
through you like a river, leave you whole.

But the greyed river, because it lacked
a certain courage, ran headlong
into the ocean waters and was gone.

Safekeeping

You never liked my thought of sharing you.
I'll go you halfers: I'm divided myself.
You with a pretty young man, you in throes,

you reaching to grip: I swear it beggars
my line that jealousy is just mental
information on steroids, nothing more,

news from the Life section, not a trespass
on rights and freedoms. I don't want to feel
more love is a gambit of zero sums.

How can we share what isn't ours to keep?
divides into *How to keep what we share?*
Never the beau I might have been, to meet

your needs I tried to cheer you on instead
to find them met. And damned if I was not
the man it took all of you to reach for.

Uttoxeter

Like a poem that makes nothing happen,
there's a story keeps coming back to me.
A winter day, seventeen eighty-one,

Dr Johnson stood in the freezing rain
and tried to extinguish a life-long regret
for having failed his father once and scorned

to pitch their wares in the marketplace.
Back he went, fifty years to the hour—
hat and wig removed, shivering with cold—

to be the person he had failed to be,
beside the one who was no longer there.
The water on his cheeks, as passers jeered,

made a real sensation, but he never moved,
and learned what lost love, love unattended,
must feel like when you didn't catch your death.

Found in an Essay by Max Beerbohm

Your old cottage was deserted.
I climbed over the gate,
walked through the long grass.

In the door-post, a small knob
of rusty iron was a mocking
reminder that to gain admission

to your house one rang the bell.
A rusty bell with no one
in sight to answer it leaves

one to go. Yet I did not go.
The movement that I made
was towards the knob itself.

I hesitated. Suppose I did
what I half meant to do
and there were no sound?

That would be ghastly.
And surely there *would* be
no sound. And if sound

there were, wouldn't that be
still worse? No footstep
of yours answering within,

making prints in the dust
out of the dark recesses,
all your inner things lasting.

My hand drew back, misgave,
suddenly closed on the knob.
I heard the scrape of the wire

—and then, faintly somewhere
deep within the heart
of your shut house, a chime.

THREE

The Natural Science of Subsequent Things

I have been passing into the next moment
for years now, as into a clearing, said the stone,
without really understanding how it happens.
I know, said the tree: the feeling each instant
of stepping off a cliff that isn't really there,
or of something being unlocked, but not by you.
For me, said the chair on the porch at evening,
it is the ease of it that stands out most.
I do nothing and yet there is this opening out.
Those verbs 'to persist' and 'to endure,'
they're all nonsense, said the river water,
and only mask what is already strange about it.
I know what you mean, said the lingering cloud,
it is like when you move in a dream
and you think the earth has been there all along,
though, when you look, it only just now
lays itself down beneath you as you drift.
I sometimes catch myself, said the mountain,
feeling like a sprinter at the finish line,
breast forward, except that I'm not moving
and there is no finish line to speak of.
I have to laugh when that happens.
It always makes me think (I tried to help)
of those automatic doors that open
just at the instant when you approach them,
except that it is the doors' opening
that makes your approaching them possible;
I wish I knew how to say it better.
I get a hard time, said the clock (ignoring me),
because people think I can tell what it is
and they can't. But I'm just here like you,
and chime in, now and then, with memories
of where I've been. I go round explaining.
Don't get me started, said the wheat field.

The daylight comes and goes. I reach out,
but my sweeping allowances only make
more room for shadows to lengthen. Not sure
where that leaves us, said the river water.
Quiet everyone, said the stone again, suddenly
stone still, as though listening for the wind.

Phobos

One evening, I was young, in my twenties,
my anxiety piqued, I was wrestling
with my ubiety's foretold termination

God knew when, as though it were a problem
to be solved with sufficient thought,
and the astonishing certainty of it—

a thing to go through, intractable,
simple as an errand—hit me so hard
and inescapably, that I bolted

from my chair, actually *stood up*, as though
to flee from my body while there was time
—'Adios, mortality thing, I'm outta here!'—

and was so embarrassed and perplexed
by having got so *actually* to my feet,
that I continued on to the kitchen, as though

to get some water, and got some water.
My body of course, iffy and spun round,
both stayed and went, the leaver and the left

pulling at a single bootstrap, a stone
figure writhing out of its half-cut block,
motion's flight from its own forward bent.

I've been getting out of chairs for years
since that day, for other reasons, but I often
think of that fretful lurch, and think too

of how light is both a particle and a wave,
depending on how you measure it, and when,
but no matter, in the end, how far it goes.

Resurrection Motif

Where is my mother, now she is gone?
Nowhere. You must think of her instead.

But where is thought exactly?
Hereabouts, but no one where anywhere.

How far is nowhere from no one where anywhere?
As near as your mother when you think of her.

Vespers

Its evening fast upon it, the poem,
always after the last word, wonders
about conclusions still to come,

and what patience might look like
if it could stop ending. It tries
to explain, but then runs out of time.

I feel for it, but most evenings
can't help but wonder if the time
after the end might be like the time

before we were, not a time when
we might have said (it went without saying)
'Life is coming now, it is soon,'

so might be, now then, no less
a waiting for what is still to come
than the time before ever was.

Continuum

If space is the illusion of time,
could I keep still and never age?
And yet I keep reaching for you.
The desire is killing me.

If time is the illusion of space,
I could simply wait long enough
and find that you were still here.
Quick, before it's too late.

Vacillating

Light is confident it appears.
It travels at its own speed.
Time, watching it go by,
stands in one place, astonished.

It was years ago that I read
the poet, sparkling with confidence,
who said we must try to go
open-eyed and laughing to the tomb.

Older and light-headed, I've stopped
trying to keep time in its proper place:
the last thing on my mind
now that I think of it, shining still.

Forest

The wind runs to tell
the young trees from the old now
lying on their sides.

Reading Biography

I

That old misgiven ruse, the book of life—
you face new chapters, turn a given page,
feel your bindings loosen—is incomplete,
a book judged too flatly by its cover.
For open the frayed tome and find within
line on line of moments all at once
pinpointing pasts and futures, if you will,
under a finger tracing each single word
from start to finish, inexorably.
You, given the finger, may not read it
more than once, may not turn forwards or back,
free, if that's the word, to follow the print's
bouncing ball to a final numbered page.
Each life's a single reading of the whole.

So far so good. Now add some Einstein,
add all you know of space-time and its twists,
a continuum that says each moment
is a *here*, like points plotted on a map,
joined by vectors of contiguity
to any distant point, whose slice of now,
let it but shift a fraction left or right
will warp across vast interstellar gaps
to intersect at angles with a time,
here at your end of things, past or to come,
where all your private onces—forward, back—
are, just think of it, somewhere else's now!
They must then in some sense still exist.
Your mother's wedding or her funeral wake,
recollected vanishments, still *take place*.

II

In one brief tableau of memory, glowed
the narrow galley kitchen's foot-wide
tiles in the old flat on Dixon Road.
A four-year-old learns at his mother's side

(she must be washing dishes at the sink),
the occult secrets of tying laces,
how to gather ends and make them link
by forming loops out of empty spaces

and bring them back around and let them pass
(while turning on the centre) into knots
twisting like wormholes through their own mass.

'It goes like this,' she says. The child amazed,
rehearses on his own, against all doubts,
the wonder of hidden ties, and is praised.

III

Take the book in hand once more and read.
Let your eyes gloss the sequent verbiage.
That sentence on page four is gone from sight,
for you who read ahead to fifty-eight,
and yet still happening, the science says,
in veiled ways that by all reading measures
are just as *there* as the late page itself,
though you can't quite put your finger on it.
Each word's a wake that, glancing, folds aside
in parting phrases, under a furrowed brow,
then opens into passing stillnesses,
just at the point of breaking, though long gone,
and also already broken, if not yet,
in the course of things. A problem for thought.

Yet readers are hardly troubled on the point.
Think of what a first page is to the last:
not gone from the book, not *not* bound as one,
just not nearly near enough to see.
But lift your eyes a moment from the page.
The book returns to its primeval state,
ungone through, whole, where in no time at all
its other nows don't so much start to be,
perhaps, as stop not being where they are,
uncancelling the written life, for us
who must finish reading. There is no end
of patience there. Call it time's wherewithal,
a knot I learned in my mother's presence
is as nearly magical as it seemed.

Over Head

I

I find myself, out of the highs
and lows, sifting love's
aimless uplifts endlessly,
wondering where they go

and what becomes of them.
That winter of 1981,
the early dark, the light country
walk north of Newmarket,

when, going steady, we stood
a moment in the narrow lane,
blizzard ablaze, the whipped-up
snowfall feathered

into whirled-off cradled
stillnesses and calms,
its luring soft spots giving way
to fetching stirs and gustos,

the silent troves above us
hanging like a sense
of our impermanence,
almost outlasting in its stay.

II

Think of it like this.
The mind's body or the body's
mind, that half-turned-
wrong-way-round pirouette

is not the flame above
a wax candle, not gilt
crown propped akimbo
over the monarch's brow.

Your brain's offspring—
the I feeling a you
as an I to be with,
each other's awareness—

is the twirling vapour
over a simmering soup,
its fine-spun wisps jostled
by kindling underheats

just at low, a hovering-above,
the sultry dewed ethers
rising a time over the mess
of potage, our birthright.

Then the final time,
when the heat shuts down,
and the vapours, come
to a head, ease off,

and the stalling ethers'
unweights, letting up,
cool soupward, their fogs
wading back into the gels

and plumbed unguents less
quickened, the mists whisked
into the liquid's liquid liquids,
the very thought of it.

III

Peace to you, dazzling blizzard.
Godspeed, hard northerlies,
your phantom hullabaloo
whirled off in new weathers.

You were something to behold.
But what fastened us spellbound
were your upheld wrap-rounds,
sashaying windwise, a buoyancy

in abeyance, waffling in hiatus,
intermission's maze so downy
in its lift, so like what love
is like that we stopped drifting,

until it must have settled surely—
the part I still can't bring to mind
to save my life—on fields of snow,
endless, as far as we could see.

Omen

It was evening that day when I was going
to be turning thirty at midnight, now
an age, I was driving home and turned
a corner onto a quiet residential street,
an early autumn evening, the birds out,
the airs of the lingering summer still warm
and the sky filling with ink towards dusk
and there was a car ahead of me and it stopped
suddenly, for a cat had gone under the tire
from between the parked cars too quickly
to see what was coming, a panic of motions,
the car ahead drove on but I got out
and I could hear the cat in the gutter by the curb,
it sounded like a wet fish flopping on a dock
and I went and looked and most of its organs
had been squeezed out and it was going to die
right then I could see but saw in my horror
how it flopped high and flopped high
with a wet sound as though it were trying
to wriggle from itself and run from what
had just happened to it, from the moment's
still pouring out in a forward way there was no
going back on, for the step taken that got him
into this bother was already taken, and then
mercifully his going through the motions
of running began to slow slowly at first
and then more quickly and a death stare
was added to his growing stillness
like an afterthought, and I wonder even now
what it must have been like to be inside him
all of you and everything just ending suddenly
in the midst of a mild evening's prowl
and there being no taking it back, only a freedom
to go through it running and running all the way

from what had happened the way it did,
or at least forward towards finding out
while he was at it where this unlikely chance
not to be gone back upon might still lead him
if he could get there. I watched him go.

Matins

Each morning I hear the truck come
from the top of the hill; the brakes wheeze
in front of my three-storey walk-up.
The beeping when it backs into the drive.

I hear the engine cut, doors open and slam,
the roll-up door at the back roll up,
men talking indifferently in twos,
a name spoken aloud, half chuckles.

Hard as I listen I can never make out
more than broken phrases:
'Not til Tuesday' and 'You don't just have.'
But one time: 'They always feel that way.'

I hear the boxes sliding on the truck floor:
two arms, two legs, two shoulders,
two knees, the single box for a torso,
two trays of fingers laid out in rows,

closed coolers marked 'Liver,'
'Kidney.' I hear 'Not that one'
and 'Two more of these.' The man
with the cooler marked 'Heart'

presses his ear to the side—'Hey fellas!'—
and pretends to listen. They laugh.
Ears in cartons that seem larger than needed.
Eyes marked 'Heavy' and 'Fragile.'

Someone drops the box with 'Brain'
marked on it and curses.
He rattles it and listens
for sounds of anything broken.

I hear their steps on the stairs.
One calls, 'What number is it again?'
It wakes me, the sudden banging at my door,
always less kind, somehow, than I hope.

Matins II

How it tired me over the years, the rising
and then the needing to send back
what came to me because it wasn't mine,

having to wind string around the bird calls
and the dawning, rolling up the exact time—
those Tuesdays at 7 a.m.—in an elastic.

I wrapped up everything, the idea of waking
and the waking itself, the bee at the screen,
the coffee cup and spoon, into the crate;

looked for something to put the chair in
and handled separately the lozenge of light
angling widely across it in the spring and fall;

packed up the tree outside at the window
laying its breezes about like a tinkerer,
the cloud above it not looking like rain,

into a box as well with the other things.
Found I grew weaker. Even the first words
drifting into my awareness of having them,

they went into a box. None for keeping,
none to have where they were. I wondered
why anyone would bother sending them,

until it came to me, the way a convalescent
remembers, slowly at first, the place of those
who had kept vigil for him, and their names.

Matins III

The morning sun's
same old same old shows
it's the earth's turn
to mimic fresh starts.

Shall I try to make one?
Mr Pope in his wisdom
said whatever is is right.
I will give him this:

that it is what it is
idles sidewise
towards the inevitable
like an asymptote.

Yet, risen from a chair,
an aging man will move
to leave his body behind
by stepping forward.

And not coming undone,
a poem angles
to wriggle free of all it's
bound to say by saying it.

So come to me at six,
Monsieur Sollay, if you like,
and watch me roll over
or rise, as I choose.

Matins IV

Right then, you should make a start. Honestly!
Look, the sun is up. Another five minutes?
You always say that. Just put up the blinds.

Every day giving some thought to your clothes,
the colours, what goes with what, remember
the coffee and the toast. Did I miss something?

How much longer will those sandals hold out?
Are you seeing Tom and Miriam after work?
I'll take the CD back, don't worry. I know …

Billie Holiday. But it sounds like a man's name.
Here's a little something in case you need it.
How should I know! You're such a character.

I agree, it's none of my business, your love life,
but it breaks my heart to imagine you
alone again this year on your birthday,

all the more when you never say a word.
I have tried, really I have. But let's be honest,
we'll never meet and I have no idea

where you are or whether you exist even.
I'm not going to be around much longer
myself, and then where will you be?

Don't be afraid. Just do like the rest of us.
We're all everyone else's everyone else.
Somehow or other, it worked for me.

Matins v

I

There's the grey beginning. Zooks!
Most nights end with a start,
it comes so quickly and so soon:
the end that is. The slate tones

dawn on you, adding themselves
to the dark the way a river changes
slowly out of backwashed inklings
that are watered down.

Caught out of doors at first light,
living it up, airing his brush
among the brothels of 15th-century
Florence, there's Brother Lippo,

Browning's painter to the life,
his understudy, his master of an art
that tells the look of things,
as like to like as like is to like.

He went for hints and glances,
a verve that favoured the living bone
over posture and stone-face,
the church's mortal absolutes.

My father too dabbled in art:
a forest path, trees by water
in pastel. Fallen barns were his forté
in pen and ink. Caricatures,

they were closer in touch to the icons
of Lippo's church than Lippo's own
semblances. They hang about me now,
make his flesh liker and his soul more like.

II

He died in a doctored sleep,
long before any made-out dawn.
The call from London came at 2 a.m.
I was on the 401 by 3,

in time to see, and yet not see,
because not looking for it,
or looking for it too late
because there seemed nothing

to find: I can think of no name
for it, save perhaps Browning's
Lippo's impromptu phrase.
Two senses of the *grey beginning*

(can you see them?) hang
like the light itself divisibly
from a single state: the dawn's final
greys easing off from the grey

itself having a point of departure,
a commencement, a moment of birth
gesturing toward the painter's
palette's still unmixed black-and-white.

Best I could hope for, I condoled,
having missed that fine line
not where the darkness comes on,
but where it ends. With an eye for living

it up and then in the sudden nick
seeing it is time, a solitary
painter slips away. *No lights! No lights!*
Your hand, sir, and goodbye.